Coming Out: Telling Family Friends

The Gallup's Guide to Modern Gay, Lesbian, & Transgender Lifestyle

BEING GAY, STAYING HEALTHY

COMING OUT:
TELLING FAMILY AND FRIENDS

FEELING WRONG IN YOUR OWN BODY:
UNDERSTANDING WHAT IT MEANS TO BE TRANSGENDER

GAY AND LESBIAN ROLE MODELS

GAY BELIEVERS:
HOMOSEXUALITY AND RELIGION

GAY ISSUES AND POLITICS:
MARRIAGE, THE MILITARY, & WORK PLACE DISCRIMINATION

GAYS AND MENTAL HEALTH:
FIGHTING DEPRESSION, SAYING NO TO SUICIDE

HOMOPHOBIA:
FROM SOCIAL STIGMA TO HATE CRIMES

HOMOSEXUALITY AROUND THE WORLD:
SAFE HAVENS, CULTURAL CHALLENGES

A NEW GENERATION OF HOMOSEXUALITY:
MODERN TRENDS IN GAY & LESBIAN COMMUNITIES

SMASHING THE STEREOTYPES:
WHAT DOES IT MEAN TO BE GAY,
LESBIAN, BISEXUAL, OR TRANSGENDER?

STATISTICAL TIMELINE AND OVERVIEW OF GAY LIFE

WHAT CAUSES SEXUAL ORIENTATION?
GENETICS, BIOLOGY, PSYCHOLOGY

GAY PEOPLE OF COLOR:
FACING PREJUDICES, FORGING IDENTITIES

GAY CHARACTERS IN THEATER, MOVIES, AND TELEVISION:
NEW ROLES, NEW ATTITUDES

Coming Out: Telling Family and Friends

by Jaime A. Seba

Mason Crest Publishers

MASON CREST PUBLISHERS INC.
370 Reed Road
Broomall, Pennsylvania 19008
(866)MCP-BOOK (toll free)
www.masoncrest.com

First Printing
9 8 7 6 5 4 3 2 1

Library of Congress Cataloging-in-Publication Data
Seba, Jaime.
  Coming out : telling family and friends / by Jaime Seba.
      p. cm.
  Includes bibliographical references and index.
  ISBN 978-1-4222-1745-0 (hardcover)   ISBN 978-1-4222-1758-0 (series)
  ISBN 978-1-4222-1865-5 (pbk.)   ISBN 978-1-4222-1863-1 (series pbk.)
  1. Coming out (Sexual orientation)—Juvenile literature. 2. Homosexuality—
Juvenile literature. 3. Gay youth—Juvenile literature. I. Title.
  HQ76.26.S43 2011
  306.76'6—dc22
                              2010017052

Produced by Harding House Publishing Service, Inc.
www.hardinghousepages.com
Interior design by MK Bassett-Harvey.
Cover design by Torque Advertising + Design.
Printed in the USA by Bang Printing

PICTURE CREDITS

City of West Hollywood, Terry Blount: p. 47
Creative Commons: pp. 14, 34, 36, 57
Dreamstime: p. 30
Light, Alan; Creative Commons: p. 17
Lowenstein, Kurt; Educational Center International Team: p. 23
Mabel, Joe; Creative Commons: p. 48
Oikawa, Kenji-Baptiste; Creative Commons: p. 33
PR Photos: p. 26
Rama; Creative Commons: p. 13
Schumin, Ben; Creative Commons: p. 11
Sykes, Bev; Creative Commons: p. 43

Contents

INTRODUCTION   6

1. WHAT IT MEANS TO COME OUT   9

2. SARAH'S STORY   29

3. ED'S STORY   39

4. SHOWING SUPPORT   51

BIBLIOGRAPHY   61

INDEX   62

ABOUT THE AUTHOR AND THE CONSULTANT   64

Introduction

We are both individuals and community members. Our differences define individuality; our commonalities create a community. Some differences, like the ability to run swiftly or to speak confidently, can make an individual stand out in a way that is viewed as beneficial by a community, while the group may frown upon others. Some of those differences may be difficult to hide (like skin color or physical disability), while others can be hidden (like religious views or sexual orientation). Moreover, what some communities or cultures deem as desirable differences, like thinness, is a negative quality in other contemporary communities. This is certainly the case with sexual orientation and gender identity, as explained in *Homosexuality Around the World*, one of the volumes in this book series.

Often, there is a tension between the individual (individual rights) and the community (common good). This is easily visible in everyday matters like the right to own land versus the common good of building roads. These cases sometimes result in community controversy and often are adjudicated by the courts.

An even more basic right than property ownership, however, is one's gender and sexuality. Does the right of gender expression trump the concerns and fears of a community or a family or a school? *Feeling Wrong in Your Own Body*, as the author of that volume suggests, means confronting, in the most personal way, the tension between individuality and community. And, while a community, family, and school have the right (and obligation) to protect its children, does the notion of property rights extend to controlling young adults' choice as to how they express themselves in terms of gender or sexuality?

Changes in how a community (or a majority of the community) thinks about an individual right or responsibility often precedes changes in the law enacted by legislatures or decided by courts. And for these changes to occur, individuals (sometimes working in small groups) often defied popular opinion, political pressure, or religious beliefs. Some of these trends are discussed in *A New Generation of Homosexuality*. Every generation (including yours!) stands on the accomplishments of our ancestors and in *Gay and Lesbian Role Models* you'll be reading about some of them.

One of the most pernicious aspects of discrimination on the basis of sexual orientation is that "homosexuality" is a stigma that can be hidden (see the volume about *Homophobia*). While some of my generation (I was your age in the early 1960s) think that life is so much easier being "queer" in the age of the Internet, Gay-Straight Alliances, and Ellen, in reality, being different in areas where difference matters is *always* difficult. Coming Out, as described in the volume of the same title, is always challenging—for both those who choose to come out and for the friends and family they trust with what was once a hidden truth. Being healthy means being honest—at least to yourself. Having supportive friends and family is most important, as explained in *Being Gay, Staying Healthy.*

Sometimes we create our own "families"—persons bound together by love and identity but not by name or bloodline. This is quite common in gay communities today as it was several generations ago. Forming families or small communities based on rejection by the larger community can also be a double-edged sword. While these can be positive, they may also turn into prisons of conformity. Does being lesbian, for example, mean everyone has short hair, hates men, and drives (or rides on) a motorcycle? *What Does It Mean to Be Gay, Lesbian, Bisexual, or Transgender?* "smashes" these and other stereotypes.

Another common misconception is that "all gay people are alike"—a classic example of a stereotypical statement. We may be drawn together because of a common prejudice or oppression, but we should not forfeit our individuality for the sake of the safety of a common identity, which is one of the challenges shown in *Gay People of Color: Facing Prejudices, Forging Identities*.

Coming out to who *you* are is just as important as having a group or "family" within which to safely come out. Becoming knowledgeable about these issues (through the books in this series and the other resources to which they will lead), feeling good about yourself, behaving safely, actively listening to others *and* to your inner spirit—all this will allow you to fulfill your promise and potential.

James T. Sears, PhD
Consultant

chapter 1

What It Means to Come Out

October 11 often seems just another day. It's not an officially recognized holiday. When it falls on a workday, banks and businesses are still open. On weekdays, school is still in session. There are no special sales in department stores, and freeways aren't jammed with holiday travelers.

But for thousands of people, it is one of the most important days of the year. It's National Coming Out Day.

"I hope that efforts such as this one will help teenagers feel that they can be themselves—and not worry that their sexual orientation may be made an obstacle to their success," Grammy Award-winning artist Melissa Etheridge said at the 2002 National Coming Out Day celebration. The theme, "Being Out Rocks," was supported by other openly *LGBT* artists

What's That Mean?

LGBT is an inclusive term used for lesbians, gays, bisexuals, and transgenders.

including Ani DiFranco, Michael Stipe, the Indigo Girls, RuPaul, and Rufus Wainwright.

The date was selected in honor of the 1987 March on Washington for Lesbian and Gay Rights, which saw a half million people participate in a demonstration in the nation's capital. It was a *pivotal* moment in the movement for gay rights, and it led *activists* Rob Eichberg and Jean O'Leary to conceive of a national Coming Out event, which began the following year. In a few short years, annual celebrations were being held in all fifty states, along with other countries around the world.

What's That Mean?

Pivotal has to do with something that is a turning point.

Activists are people who are committed to social change through political and personal action.

"Coming out" is defined by the Human Rights Campaign (HRC), an LGBT advocacy group, as "the process in which a person first acknowledges, accepts and appreciates his or her sexual orientation or gender identity and begins to share with others." It is an incredibly important personal journey that means something different for each individual.

The HRC identifies three main stages to this complicated process. The first is Opening Up to Yourself, when individuals fully recognize and accept that they are gay, lesbian, or bisexual. As with each of the stages, this takes a different amount of time for each person. Some people may reach personal acceptance when they are still children, while others may not acknowledge their sexuality until they are adults.

Once someone comes to terms with her own identity, she'll need to take careful thought and consideration to begin the second stage, which is called Coming Out. This is the time when people are actively discussing their sexual orientation for the first time with important people in their lives. For some, this may happen multiple times. People may come out to friends first, but wait years before telling their families.

In 2009, National Coming Out Day was celebrated with a march on Washington, D.C., in which hundreds of thousands participated.

After working through the first two stages, people are finally able to begin Living Openly. Once their friends and families are aware of their orientation, gay people then make the personal choice of how much it will impact their lives. This is the ongoing part of the process that varies significantly, depending on the individual. Some people continue to keep their personal lives private, accepting their sexual orientation as only a minor part of their overall identity. Others, like Adrienne Hudek, embrace their new gay lifestyle in a much bigger way.

"After I came out, it was all about rainbow pride," said Adrienne, referring to the gay pride symbol of the rainbow flag. She came out to her friends and family when she was twenty-one. "I participated in pride marches, volunteered for gay organization, took part in protests, had rainbow bumper stickers on my car, everything. I couldn't wait to tell people I was gay, whether they needed to know or not!"

That enthusiasm is not uncommon among young gay people, and it is often the celebration at the end of a long journey, with many roadblocks and struggles along the way. To provide assistance during the stages of Coming Out, the HRC distributes a *Resource Guide to Coming Out*. The guide makes clear that when coming out, it's normal to feel scared, vulnerable, brave, proud, confused, relieved, and uncertain—all at the same time.

Gay pride is a movement that affirms LGBT identity. It has three main premises: that people should be proud of their sexual orientation and gender identity, that diversity is a gift, and that sexual orientation and gender identity are inherent and cannot be intentionally altered.

"When I made the decision to come out, I felt about a hundred emotions all at once," said Adrienne. "It was so exciting, so scary, so invigorating. I knew my whole life was going to change."

Compared to many people, Adrienne's coming out process didn't seem very difficult. The first person she told was her openly gay roommate, Brad. But even though she knew he would obviously under-

Adolescence is a difficult time for many individuals, a time when establishing one's own identity as separate from one's parents can be stressful and full of conflict. For LGBT teenagers, the challenges of adolescence can be even greater.

stand, she was still worried about the impact her announcement would have on him.

"It sounds weird to be afraid to come out to someone who's gay, but I really wondered if it would change things, because liking guys was something he thought we had in common!" she said. "But it was more than that. This was the first step. And I wanted to take fifteen more steps, but at the same time I was scared of what would come next. So I needed this to go well so that I would have the courage to keep going."

She thought about it for days, wrote drafts of what she would say, practiced in front of a mirror, and imagined the different reactions he might have. Finally, the day came.

"I was so nervous that it took me a few minutes to get it out. He was very patient, and he waited for me to say it. And then he just laughed," she said with a smile. "He gave me a hug and said, 'Yeah, I already knew that. It's pretty obvious.' And then he went back to working on his computer. It was no big deal. That made me feel much more confident about telling other people."

The love and acceptance from her friends allowed Adrienne to get to the next step, which was telling her parents. Though her mother had always been open-minded and supportive about gay issues and causes, Adrienne didn't know if that would apply to their real lives, too. She had friends whose parents seemed *liberal* and forward-thinking, until it came to their own children being gay.

"I knew a guy whose parents were always talking about equal rights for everyone and loving your neighbor and being a good Christian," she said. "So he thought it would be no big deal to tell them he was gay. He was sure they would understand and even be happy that he told them. But when he did, they went crazy. They said he was just trying to get attention, and that it was only a phase. They told him if he was going to be gay, then he couldn't live in their house. So he had to leave home when he was sixteen. I couldn't have handled that."

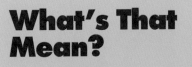

What's That Mean?

To be *liberal* is to be open to new ideas and accepting and supportive of these ideas.

Fortunately, she didn't have to. Just as Adrienne hoped, her mother simply listened, asked a few questions, and let Adrienne know she was loved. Then they talked about dating, just as they always had. Adrienne's only regret was that she didn't accept herself earlier, so she could have come out even sooner.

"I look around now and see these kids who are eleven or twelve years old, and they are living completely out," she said. "People wonder how they can know at that age, but I knew. And I wonder what my life would have been like if I'd come out when I was that young. It's different for everyone, and you have to go at your own pace. But I really admire these kids, and their parents and friends who accept them, because they get to grow up knowing who they are."

Nationally, there has been a trend of young people coming out at an earlier age than ever before. At least 120 middle schools across the country have gay-straight alliance (GSA) groups. These student organizations, which are also in more than 4,000 high schools, provide gay and lesbian teens and their straight peers with a safe environment in which to meet. Every year at prom season, newspapers across the country carry stories of same-sex couples attending school dances, and community organizations hold Gay Proms for LGBT teens.

"This is the first generation of gay kids who have the great joy of being able to argue with their parents

Actress Ellen Degeneres has spoken out strongly in support of LGBT teens' right to participate in proms and other school events.

about dating, just like their straight peers do," said Ritch Savin-Williams, professor of developmental psychology at Cornell University.

EXTRA INFO

Hate crimes occur when a perpetrator targets a victim because of his or her membership in a certain social group, usually a racial group, religion, sexual orientation, disability, nationality, age, or gender identity. The term usually refers to criminal acts motivated by hatred. The crimes include physical assault, damage to property, bullying, harassment, verbal abuse or insults, offensive graffiti, or hate mail.

Policymakers in many nations and at all levels of government have become more concerned about hate crimes in recent years, but these crimes are not new. The Romans persecuted the early Christians; the Ottomans slaughtered the Armenians; the Nazis sent millions of Jews and others to the crematoriums; and more recently, the ethnic cleansing in Bosnia and the genocide in Rwanda horrified the world. Hate crimes have shaped the world's history.

In the United States, racial and religious prejudice has inspired most hate crimes. As Europeans began to colonize the New World in the sixteenth and seventeenth centuries, Native tribes increasingly became the targets of intimidation and violence. After the Civil War, the Ku Klux Klan and other hate groups lynched African Americans. The Klan's hate targets included lesbian, gay, bisexual, and transgender people.

Thanks to strong relationships with family and friends, young people like Adrienne have coming out experiences that are very positive. But that is not always the case. In fact, many people never come out or delay making the decision because they fear what will happen as a result. People have thousands of reasons for not making the decision to come out, and one of the biggest is not being accepted by friends, family members, or churches.

"I couldn't imagine what my parents or family would say if they found out about these feelings," said Sarah Carlin, who came out while still in high school. "My dad always joked and called gay people 'queers.' My mom was no better."

Like many parents, Sarah's mom and dad made anti-gay remarks without giving it much thought. They never considered the possibility that Sarah was a lesbian, and so they were never concerned about the impact these statements could have on her when she was growing up. That mindset is not uncommon, but it can be changed through education and awareness. Organizations such as Parents, Families and Friends of Lesbians and Gays (PFLAG) provide support and information from people who have been through this process with a loved one themselves.

As part of its Coming Out Project, the HRC recognizes other risks. In some states, people can be fired from their jobs for being gay. Gay people may be the victims of intolerance or hate crimes from peers and family members who don't understand or approve. Young people have even been thrown out of their homes or physically abused for being gay. A report from the National Gay and Lesbian Task Force shows that a *disproportionate* number of homeless young people in America are homosexual.

In light of these very real possibilities, people need to fully consider the *repercussions* of coming out and take advantage of the support that is available. Teachers and guidance counselors, supportive spiritual leaders, therapists, gay friends, and LGBT hotlines can all be valuable resources for gay people who are taking the first steps.

Considering the pitfalls and challenges, some may wonder why people feel the need to come out at all. Why do people put themselves through such difficult and even *traumatic* experiences? One reason is because staying hidden away, "in the closet," can

What's That Mean?

Disproportionate means an overrepresentation of a particular group within a larger group.

Repercussions are results and reactions that are often negative.

Something that is *traumatic* is a strongly negative experience that can have a long-lasting effect on a person.

be even more damaging. A 1998 study showed that lesbians who disclosed their sexuality to friends and family were more content in their personal lives and were less likely to engage in harmful behavior. Conversely, individuals who remain closeted or who are forced to keep their sexuality a secret are more at risk for suicide and depression.

"Most of the emotional disturbance experienced by gay men and lesbians around their sexual identity is not based on physiological causes but rather is due more to a sense of **alienation** in an unaccepting environment," the American Medical Association stated in 1994.

Until the gay rights movement gained significant momentum in the 1960s and 1970s, LGBT people were often forced to stay hidden and convince those around them that they were actually straight. For many, this even included getting married and having children. Otherwise, they risked losing their income, their families, and even their homes. And for many people, those times have not yet passed. Despite the many advances in awareness of LGBT issues, these threats to an LGBT person's happiness and civil rights still exist today.

As a result, it can take decades for closeted people to come out even to themselves, and much longer to come out to the world, if they are ever able. And that can include people coming out to their wives or husbands and children. Many therapists who assist adults in the coming out process caution their patients about rushing through the stages too quickly, without fully considering the effect they will have on their lives and families.

"We're careful to not say to people, 'Come out immediately'—that's not realistic," said Chris Kraft, clinical director at the Johns Hopkins Sexual Behaviors Consultation Unit.

Organizations have been formed to help provide resources to those who come out later in life. In the 1980s, people recognized the need for gay parents to find support and advocacy. The result was Children of Lesbians and Gays Everywhere (COLAGE), which supplies parents with information on how best to come out to their children. And Seniors Active in a Gay Environment (SAGE) provides resources and support to older gay individuals, including information and assistance on topics from health care to housing.

There are also good reasons for LGBT people to consider coming out that go beyond personal self-respect and individual happiness. If every LGBT person came out, prejudice and oppression against LGBT people might simply cease to exist, since everyone already

"The closet" is a metaphor for what GLBT individuals experience when they cannot reveal their true identities: a cramped, hidden existence where they have no room to grow or explore possibilities. "Coming out of the closet" can be frightening—but it also opens up opportunities for people to be true to themselves and discover their own potential.

knows, loves, and respects an LGBT person, whether they know it or not! By coming out, by identifying themselves, families and friends of LGBT people are forced to confront their own prejudices toward a "group" to which their own child, their own sibling, their own parent, or their own friend belongs. So an individual's coming out has an important social and political effect, too. Multiplied by thousands, by tens of thousands, by millions, the process of a single LGBT person coming out to people who know and love him can make the world a better place for all LGBT people.

At a political level, this has led to a movement by some LGBT activists to publicly "out" famous people—celebrities, professional athletes, actors, prominent business people, religious leaders, and politicians—in order to force them to take a step for the "good of the community." Especially in the area of politics and religion, some of these closeted people, because of their own fears and self-hatred, have been some of the worst enemies of the LGBT community, supporting discrimination and holding back the movement for full civil rights for LGBT people.

But while coming out is very important to the progress of the LGBT community the privacy of those people who choose not to come out is also important. Some people come from families or live in communities where coming out would literally be threatening to their lives. Others engage in "gay"

EXTRA INFO

LGBT youth are coming out younger than ever before. Recent studies have shown that the average age for gay and lesbian young people to begin the process of coming out is now 16; back in the 1980s, it was between 19 and 23. This means that many more young people are coming out when they are still at school, which can seriously impact their school and home lives. Another study found that half of students who experience homophobia and bullying have skipped school because of it. Schools that openly acknowledge and include LGBT students, and are outspoken about opposing bullying, create a positive environment in which all students feel safe and able to learn.

For many young people, coming out as LGBT can also mean risking rejection and even the loss of support from family. As young people are less likely to have financial resources to support themselves if they are cut off from their families, this can lead to considerable hardship, including homelessness, mental health problems, and substance abuse. In the United States, LGBT young people represent a disproportionate number of homeless youth: between 20 and 40 percent.

sexual behavior, either occasionally or exclusively, but because of their cultural background or community of origin would never label themselves as LGBT. Whatever their reasons, people have the right to make their own decisions. To take this right from them is an act of invasion.

Ricky Martin was repeatedly pushed by interviewers (including Barbara Walters in a televised interview) to admit that he was gay. He denied it until 2010, when he made the decision to publically come out. "I am very blessed to be who I am," he wrote on his website.

No one is immune to the complex tensions involved with coming out. Even celebrities must ask themselves the same questions and face the same issues as everyone else who considers taking such a big step. But many of them must do it on a national or global stage. Singer Ricky Martin was an international superstar when rumors that he might be gay began to appear in news stories and gossip columns. But he never came out publicly for fear of how it would impact his career, reputation, public perception, and family life. It took years for him to take that step, which he finally did in 2010. In a statement on his website, he wrote about what he referred to as his personal truth, and the influence his children had on inspiring him to finally leave the closet.

"(The truth) fills me with strength and courage," Martin said. "This is just what I need especially now that I am the father of two beautiful boys that are so full of light and who, with their outlook, teach me new things every day. To keep living as I did up until today would be to indirectly diminish the glow that my kids were born with. . . . These years in silence and reflection made me stronger and reminded me that acceptance has to come from within and that this kind of truth gives me the power to conquer emotions I didn't even know existed."

FIND OUT MORE ON THE INTERNET

The American Gay Rights Movement: A Short History
civilliberty.about.com/od/gendersexuality/tp/
History-Gay-Rights-Movement.htm

Ricky Martin Music Official Website.
rickymartinmusic.com

READ MORE ABOUT IT

Huegal, Kelly, *GLBTQ: The Survival Guide for Queer and Questioning Teens*. Minneapolis, Minn.: Free Spirit Publishing, 2007.

Trachtenberg, Robert, editor. *When I Knew*. New York: HarperCollins, 2005.

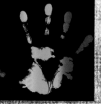

chapter 2

Sarah's Story

Like most little girls, Sarah Carlin enjoyed playing with her Barbie dolls. She kept a diary. She spied on older kids in the neighborhood and looked forward to growing up.

She also started to have feelings that she knew made her different.

When she was about nine years old, her family lived across the street from the small local high school. She would sit on her porch and watch two girls sneak outside the school and kiss. "For some reason I was so intrigued," she said. "I wondered why they had to sneak around. I was so confused because my mom and dad had never told me about two girls or two boys kissing."

Sarah had already begun to recognize her interest in other girls, though her highest level of experimentation had been having her Barbie dolls kiss each other. But it was enough to make her identify with the girls she saw.

She wasn't alone. Increasingly, gay youth are coming out earlier than ever before. Studies show that people begin to experience sexual attraction between the ages of ten and twelve, when straight little boys begin to notice little girls.

"No one says to them: 'Are you sure? You're too young to know if you like girls. It's probably just a phase,'" said Eileen Ross, the director of the Outlet Program, a support service for gay youth in Mountain View, California. "But that's what we say too often to gay youth. We deny them their feelings and truth in a way we would never do with a heterosexual young person."

Depression is more common in young adults who are rejected by their families because of their sexual identities—and depression can contribute to other serious problems, including drug abuse and suicide.

The repercussions of such a response can be severe. Caitlin Ryan, a researcher at San Francisco State University, spent more than seven years studying the link between how families respond to a gay child coming out and the child's mental health in early adulthood. She found that when teens were rejected by their families, they were more likely to have attempted suicide, used drugs, or suffered depression than those raised by families who accepted them. The "rejecting behaviors" identified by the study included verbal and physical abuse, using derogatory terms for gay people, and forbidding their children to associate with other gay and lesbian youth.

Sarah experienced those behaviors firsthand when her mother saw the same two girls kissing. Sarah was deeply impacted by her reaction.

"She saw the two girls and said, 'Ugh! Girls kissing is not right! That's gross, Sarah!'" she said. "I didn't know why, but I felt ashamed and sad. It was like I had to give up something within myself. That is probably when I began to really try my hardest to push any feelings of liking a girl out of my head."

In an effort to fit in with the straight kids at school, Sarah did what many young people do when faced with rejection by their parents. She had boyfriends in middle school and high school, and she tried to be a typical straight girl. But the more she tried to be "normal," the more she felt the negative effects on her life.

"I was so sad because I didn't want this, but I knew it was what I had to do and be," she said.

Then in her junior year of high school, she learned one of her friends was a lesbian. So was her favorite teacher. Finally, she wasn't alone anymore. There were people who understood. There were people who were just like her.

"She became my *mentor*," Sarah said of her teacher. "I felt like she could know about me and could maybe even help me. She told me that there was a life out there, outside of my class of ninety-seven kids, and that I could be who I was. I felt relieved but so scared. I made a plan to go to college and then tell my mom and dad over the phone—and then hang up on them. That is not what happened."

What's That Mean?

A *mentor* is someone who teaches and offers support to, often, a younger person.

At the time, Sarah was being treated for depression and an eating disorder, and she had come to rely on and trust her therapist. She needed support, so she overcame her fear and decided to come out to her therapist, a common first step for many gay and lesbian people.

"I went in and almost threw up, I was so nervous," she said.

Unable to say the words, she wrote, "I think I'm gay" on a piece of paper, folded it over and over again,

Straight parents may be uncomfortable seeing public displays of affection between same-sex teen couples, even though they would consider those same behaviors perfectly acceptable and normal between straight teens.

and finally handed it to her therapist. She waited for a response, unable to make eye contact, terrified at what the reaction would be.

"My therapist opened the piece of paper and shook her head and kind of chuckled," Sarah said. "She said, 'Sarah, I've been waiting for you to tell me because I already knew. Your mother called here about two months ago, saying that she had read your journal and thought you were gay.'"

Sarah was furious that her privacy had been violated. She felt betrayed by her own parents. Though she wanted to continue with her plan and remain closeted until she left home for college, she was overcome by emotion and couldn't contain it. When her mother picked her up from the therapist's office, Sarah confronted her with the truth.

"She looked like she had just seen a ghost," Sarah said. "I began crying and so did she."

It was a barrage of emotion and statements that experts like Eileen Ross have come to know well. *That's not how we raised you. How did this happen? It's not right. It's just a phase. You'll outgrow it.* Though it only lasted for about ten minutes, it was a turning point in Sarah's life.

"I wanted scream at her, but I couldn't find my voice," Sarah said. "I don't remember much except for being miserable for about a year."

For the rest of her time in high school, Sarah struggled with finding her way out of the closet on her own. Without the benefit of a Gay-Straight Alliance at her school, she confided in a few trusted friends and teachers because she didn't feel ready to come out completely. She didn't know what would happen if other people knew.

"I went to a small high school and was scared for my safety if I came out," she said.

PFLAG (Parents, Families, and Friends of Lesbians and Gays) is an organization that helps parents accept and support their LGBT children.

Sexual orientation is still one of the most common targets of school bullying, but more and more schools are developing zero-tolerance policies toward any bullying or harassment in their halls.

She had good reason to be concerned. In a survey conducted by the Gay, Lesbian, and Straight Education Network (GLSEN) in 2007, 81 percent of LGBT middle school students reported being regularly **harassed** at school because of their sexual orientation and 39 percent were physically assaulted. Even worse, only 29 percent of those who reported bullying to school officials felt it was handled effectively. When there is no support at school, young people rely even more on their families. In Sarah's case, though, that wasn't much of an option.

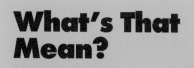

What's That Mean?

Harassed means that someone is teased, bullied, or physically threatened on an ongoing basis.

"My dad didn't really speak to me for a while," she said. "He acted like he would 'catch the gayness' if he got too close."

Eventually, her mother started to become more informed. She attended PFLAG meetings with Sarah, met Sarah's gay friends, and gradually became more accepting.

"But still, to this day, she doesn't say 'gay,'" Sarah said. "She calls it 'that way.'"

Over time, Sarah's relationship with her parents improved. She went to college, began dating, and lived openly, embracing her sexual identity. She recognizes how brave it is for young people to come out in high school. And she offers some advice.

"Whenever they come out, it has to be when *they* decide," she said. "But no matter what, they need to know that they can be happy and be themselves."

FIND OUT MORE ON THE INTERNET

Anti-Gay Discrimination in Schools: Teaching Tolerance
www.tolerance.org/activity/anti-gay-discrimination-schools

READ MORE ABOUT IT

Gold, Mitchell and Wendy Drucker. *Crisis: 40 Stories Revealing the Personal, Social, and Religious Pain and Trauma of Growing Up Gay in America*. Austin, Tex.: Greenleaf, 2008.

Human Rights Watch. *Hatred in the Hallways: Violence and Discrimination Against Lesbian, Gay, Bisexual and Transgender Students in U.S. Schools*. New York: Human Rights Watch, 2001.

chapter 3

Ed's Story

From the time he was a teenager, Ed Wesley knew he was gay. He had his first boyfriend when he was eighteen, and he attempted his first step toward coming out when he was twenty-one.

That's when he confided in his campus minister, who recommended that Ed tell his parents and then go to an ex-gay ministry.

"They treated it like it was an addiction," said Ed. "They told me it was not in God's plan for me."

The reaction was crushing to Ed, a devout Christian who prized his spiritual life above all else. The notion that being gay was a sin or against the will of God forced him back in the closet.

It was nearly fifteen years before he tried again. At 2 p.m. on October 5, 2005, Ed finally took that big leap.

"It was my thirty-fifth birthday," he said. "And I had the realization that I didn't want to live the next thirty-five years like I had for the first thirty-five."

EXTRA INFO

Evangelical Christians against same-sex marriages are convinced that homosexuality is a sin. Here is a summary of their perspectives, written by the Christian Family Law Association:

If we assume, for the sake of argument, that a person could have a gene that produces a tendency toward a particular behavior, does the presence of such a genetic tendency justify the behavior? One might argue that God made me that way, and since he does not make mistakes, he must have intended that I act in accordance with my genetic tendency. But such a view ignores what the Bible has to say about man's fallen and sinful nature. It also ignores the idea that there are absolute moral truths that have governed society and behaviors since ancient times. Basing our laws on [genetic tendencies] would mean that we should accept all forms of greed, pedophilia, sadomasochism, and other destructive behaviors to which people can be genetically inclined. Our innate desires or tendencies, even genetic tendencies, must not be confused with God's will for our identities to be moral, righteous, and consistent with biblical truth. An innate desire or tendency may be morally appropriate and lawful in one context, yet highly immoral and unlawful in another. For instance, an innate tendency for sexual arousal with a spouse is considered morally appropriate and lawful, while sexual arousal with a child is not only immoral but criminal. We can conclude that although we are not morally responsible for having a particular genetic tendency or desire, we are morally responsible for what we act on and do.

(From "A Christian Perspective on Same-Sex Relationships," www.christianfamilylawassociation.org/same-sex_relationships)

Ed's experience was very similar to thousands of other gay people when they first attempt the difficult process of coming out. In fact, many wait much longer to embrace their identity. According to Chris Kraft, the clinical director at the Johns Hopkins Sexual Behaviors Consultation Unit, men who decide to come out late in adulthood have often known about their sexual orientation since their youth but did not want to risk telling others. One of the biggest reasons for this is the effect it will have on their families, as well as the prospect of being faced with intolerance from the people closest to them, just as Ed experienced.

"I was always afraid I was going to lose the love of my parents, and that I wouldn't be allowed to come home again if they knew I was gay," he said. "They always said I could tell them anything, but the one time I tried, the reaction they had made me close up."

Those fears have kept many people in the closet for their entire lives. But as gay rights issues grab headlines in the news, and gay characters increasingly appear in movies and on television, thousands of people have made the decision to come out late in life. Filmmakers Beatrice Alda and her wife, Jennifer Brooke, created the 2008 documentary *Out Late* to capture the experiences of people who wait until their golden years to embrace their sexual identity.

"For me, the message is, you have one life, and if you can find a way to get to be who you really are before life ends, that's a gift," says Alda, who married Brooke in Canada in 2006.

For years, Ed was told that he couldn't be gay and still have the most important thing in his life—his faith. So he stayed in the closet. Even when he travelled as a consultant in education, he still couldn't be himself. What would his family say? What would happen to his career? He had been honored with a Parent's Choice Award for his performing art. What would they think if they knew he was gay?

Those questions haunted him so much that he didn't have romantic relationships and didn't explore what it meant to be gay. For more than a decade, denying who he was left a gaping hole in his life.

Sometimes people in the GLBT community wait entire lifetimes before they claim their full identities. These two women waited 31 years to be together legally, and in 2005, their state of California allowed them to marry.

While in graduate school in the spring of 2005, Ed was studying a form of therapy when he heard something that stuck with him. "If you're not happy," the professor said, "you need to change something."

A short time later, Ed had completed his master's degree, a notable personal success—and he was thinking about suicide. He sat in church, surrounded by a mass of friendly people, and he felt lonely and isolated. When he watched television and listened to music, he heard constantly all about other people's love—heterosexual love. He felt lost, out of place, and angry.

"It didn't make sense to me. Why would God want me to suffer?" he said.

As he celebrated his birthday and reflected on the previous thirty-five years, he shook his fist at God in fury. Then he got down on his knees and took the most important step he could to come out. But he wasn't coming out to his family, his friends, or even his minister. This was much more personal.

"I was coming out to God. I was telling God who I was," Ed said. "I thought about the pain of the past. I had spent all that time denying myself the opportunity to love another person because I couldn't love myself. And I couldn't love myself because I thought God didn't love me the way I was."

He turned to a friend, a spiritual confidante whom Ed had known since his childhood. He took a deep breath, carefully chose his words, and finally told his friend what he had been waiting more than a decade to express out loud. He never expected what he heard in return.

"I told him I was gay, and he said he was, too," Ed said. "I was stunned, just stunned."

His friend was older than Ed. He was married with children. He continued to be active in his church, and he lived the life that was expected of him. He was happy, but he had many regrets. And he didn't want to see his good friend take the same path.

"He told me not to make the same mistakes he did," Ed said. "That really had an effect on me. It made me see everything differently."

When he recognized the impact that denying himself could have on his life, his decision was clear. He knew what he had to do. He just wasn't sure how to do it.

That fall he accepted a position teaching computer classes on a cruise ship. At sea, away from his home and the ties to his past, Ed decided he was going to live his life out loud and proud.

"My friend told me that you have to be comfortable in your own skin before anyone else will accept you," he said. "That's so true. Working on ships represented the opportunity for me to live openly and not have it matter at all. I could be who I was, and nobody cared."

That experience helped him to accept himself fully. But he still wasn't quite sure what it meant to be gay. He hadn't known many gay people, and he only had images on television and in movies. And they didn't quite look like him.

"Those guys are handsome models with perfect bodies. I'm a big guy," said Ed, who has a husky frame, bald-shaved head, and a goatee. "We don't have gay role models, gay fathers who can mentor us. We don't have ordinary-looking guys who are like us on TV or in movies. That makes it very difficult to find an image of a gay person we can relate to."

While in Los Angeles on a business trip, Ed turned to two of his friends. Both openly gay, they offered the support, wisdom, and assistance he had been missing all those years.

"They basically gave me gay culture lessons," he said with a smile. "We went to West Hollywood, the gay area of LA, and I'd never seen anything like it before. There was no judgment. You could be gay, and it didn't matter to anyone."

Ed felt so comfortable in that environment that about a year later he relocated to the Los Angeles area. He put a rainbow sticker on his car, became active in the community, and was finally comfortable in his own skin. It didn't take long for him to begin a relationship, his first in nearly twenty years.

Southern California's West Hollywood is an openly gay community, where restaurants and clubs demonstrate gay pride.

Not all churches reject homosexuals. Many in the Christian faith affirm their welcome to everyone, allowing GLBT individuals to integrate their faith and their lifestyle.

And the most important part of his life is thriving. He has a deep and meaningful relationship with God, which he can express openly. His church home welcomes everyone. The words "You're accepted here" are emblazoned all over their publications. And Ed expresses his faith by playing the drums in the church band and singing hymns of praise. He can truly be himself—a devoted Christian, a successful professional, a productive member of the community, and a gay man.

He still returns home to Kentucky to visit his parents. He has never formally come out to his parents, not after the first time when he was twenty-one. His mother continues to mention him having kids and getting married.

"I think my parents know, but they've never accepted it," he said. "I'm still Ed Wesley. The fact that I'm a gay man doesn't change anything. And I have to respect their opinion and not force them to accept me."

While it isn't perfect, Ed is content with knowing that other members of his family know he's gay and accept him. And, more important, he accepts himself.

"No one ever asked me if I wanted to be gay," he said. "It definitely would have been a lot easier for me if I was straight, in terms of my family, church, business. But I am gay. And I spent many years trying to be somebody I'm not. I think about how different my life would have been. But that's in the past. This is where I am now, and my life is complete."

FIND OUT MORE ON THE INTERNET

Homosexuality and Religion Resources
hirr.hartsem.edu/research/homosexuality_religion.html

Religious Tolerance
www.religioustolerance.org/hom_chur.htm

READ MORE ABOUT IT

De la Juerta, Christian. *Coming Out Spiritually: The Next Step*. New York: Tarcher, 2009.

Johnson, Toby. *Gay Spirituality*. Maple Shade, N.J.: Lethe Press, 2004.

Rogers, Jack. *Jesus, the Bible, and Homosexuality: Explode the Myths, Heal the Church*. Louisville, Ken.: Westminster John Knox, 2009.

chapter 4

Showing Support

In 1972, Jeanne Manford proudly joined her gay son, Morty, as he marched in New York's Pride Day parade. She was surprised when gay and lesbian people she'd never met came up to her and asked for her assistance in speaking with their own parents. She immediately saw a need for support.

So the following spring, she organized the first meeting of a support group for parents whose children had come out. The session was held at a local church and was attended by about twenty people.

More than thirty-five years later, that small group has grown into Parents, Families and Friends of Lesbians and Gays. The organization, now commonly known as PFLAG, has more than 200,000 members meeting in thousands chapters all over the country. In those meetings, most parents begin the same way Manford did. They are just showing their support or seeking to understand their gay and lesbian children.

"It's parental. It's an instinctual response to protect their own children," said Ron Schlittler, former PFLAG deputy executive director. "So many parents are not born activists. They don't come by this naturally."

In fact, many parents who never would have considered themselves activists or spokespeople find themselves suddenly in that role when they seek to support their gay children. That was the case for Betty DeGeneres. Her daughter, actress/comedian Ellen DeGeneres, made headlines around the world in 1997 when she came out publicly on her primetime sitcom. It didn't take long for her mother to become part of the story, and Betty recognized the significance of her new role.

"The fact that I'm a mom **advocating** equal rights for my daughter and her partner underscores the point that ending discrimination based on sexual orientation is not just important to gay people, it's important to their families and the people who love them," she told *HRC Quarterly* in 1997.

What's That Mean?

Advocating means standing up for someone or something.

Discrimination is when someone is treated differently because of his or her race, sexual identity, religion, or some other factor.

That year, she became the first straight spokesperson for National Coming Out Day.

"For too long, gay Americans have suffered **discrimination**," she said in a televised public service announcement that coincided with the annual event. "As long as our sons and daughters are excluded from the basic protection of law, we must share that burden as a family."

When coming out, gay people often turn to their friends for support first, especially among younger people. One reason for this is that younger people tend to be more accepting of gay people. A Gallup Poll in 2007 showed that 54 percent of Americans found homosexuality acceptable, but it was nearly 10 percent higher for people ages 18-29.

"You're not friends with someone just because they're straight, so why wouldn't you be friends with someone if they're gay?" asked Mollie Sachs. "It's just part of who they are." Mollie is straight and married, but she has numerous colleagues and close friends who are openly gay. Though she has never had a family member come out to her, she's **empathizes** with what the experience must be like. But she also knows it would never change the way she feels about someone she loves.

What's That Mean?

Someone who **empathizes** feels for another person; she puts herself mentally and emotionally in the other person's place.

"I can understand why some people might be surprised if they find out their friend or family member is gay," she said. "It can have a big impact on a person's life. But if you accept someone, then you accept everything about them. You can't pick and choose."

When a gay person decides to come out, their supportive friends and family often want to help make the process easier. But they don't know how. The most important thing that straight people can do for their gay friends and family members is to learn more about what it means to be homosexual. The HRC, in partnership with PFLAG, provides *A Straight Guide to GLBT Americans*. The booklet is designed to provide information to people who have recently learned that a friend or family member is gay.

> Maybe you always suspected. Maybe it's a total surprise. But no matter what, the moment a friend, loved one or acquaintance makes the decision to come out and tell you about being gay, lesbian, bisexual or transgender, it is always a unique event. For a lot of people, learning that someone they know and care about is GLBT can open a range of emotions, from confused to concerned, awkward to honored. It may be hard to know how to react—leaving you with

EXTRA INFO

One. Build the capacity of our organization at every level so that we may have all the resources, in the form of information, people and funding, necessary to move forward in our work with the greatest possible effect.

Two. Create a world in which our young people may grow up and be educated with freedom from fear of violence, bullying and other forms of discrimination, regardless of their real or perceived gender identity or sexual orientation or that of their families.

Three. Make our vision and our message accessible to the broadest range of ethnic and cultural communities, ending the isolation of families with lesbian, gay, bisexual and transgender family members within those communities.

Four. Work toward full inclusion of lesbian, gay, bisexual and transgender persons within their chosen communities of faith.

Five. Create a society in which all LGBT persons may openly and safely pursue the career path of their choice, and may be valued and encouraged to grow to their full potential in the workplace.

Six. Create a society in which all lesbian, gay, bisexual and transgender persons may enjoy, in every aspect of their lives, full civil and legal equality and may participate fully in all the rights, privileges and obligations of full citizenship in this country.

questions about what to say, how to talk about being GLBT and wanting to know what you can do to be supportive.

The guide recommends that people ask questions and be honest. This not only communicates interest and understanding, but also support. Many people respond initially with confusion, shock, or even anger and fear. But by talking about it and learning more, they can reach an understanding and even be a source of support and comfort for gay friends. The HRC also offers suggestions for ways people can demonstrate their support, including:

- Create social settings that bring together your straight and GLBT friends and family.

- Find opportunities to talk openly with your straight friends about your GLBT friends and family and the issues that they face.

- Make sure that you include the same-sex partner of your GLBT loved one in events and activities just as you would any other friend's spouse or significant other.

- Don't allow anti-GLBT jokes or statements expressed in your presence to go unchal-lenged.

- Find out if your employer has an equal-rights policy — and if not, encourage the organization's leadership to adopt one.

- Many companies have employee resource groups with policies that include GLBT employees. ERGs can be very helpful in giving you ways to show support at work.

- Research the views of candidates for public office and factor their stand on GLBT equality into your voting decisions.

Parents and siblings of GLBT individuals show their support in a gay pride parade in Mexico City.

What's That Mean?

Vitriol is a strong, hostile reaction, often expressed in the written word.

Controversy is a situation where differing opinions create tension and strong reactions.

The key to offering support to someone who is coming out is to respect the individual's feelings and privacy. This includes recognizing if someone hasn't actually made the choice to come out. What is commonly known as "outing" occurs when someone other than the gay person discloses that he or she is homosexual. Outing takes the power of decision-making and control away from the individual; it leaves the person feeling confused, betrayed, and embarrassed. In many cases, someone may have discovered an individual's sexual orientation and decided to announce it to others.

Actor Neil Patrick Harris encountered just such a situation when his sexual orientation became the source of much speculation in the media. Though he had been living openly in his private life for years, he had decided not to publicly come out. But as rumors spread that he was gay, many people became frustrated that he did not speak out as an advocate for gay rights.

"The Internet stuff threw me for a loop because I didn't understand where the **vitriol** was coming from," Harris said. "I thought I had been representing well, and in turn it seemed like I was quickly condemned to step to the plate."

Though frustrated by the pressure, attention, and **controversy**, Harris finally decided to make a public statement about his sexuality in 2006:

> The public eye has always been kind to me, and until recently I have been able to live a pretty normal life. Now it seems there is speculation and interest in my private life and relationships. So, rather than ignore those who choose to publish their opinions without actually talking to me, I am happy to dispel any rumors or misconceptions and am quite proud to say that I am a very content gay man living my life to the fullest and feel most fortunate to be working with wonderful people in the business I love.

Regardless of the circumstances, the way friends and family react when someone comes out has a significant impact on a gay person's self-esteem and self-confidence. People must decide for themselves how they want to respond. But to Sarah Carlin, who relied heavily on her close friends when she came out in high school, the matter is simple.

"Stay true to your friends," she said. "They were your friends before you knew they were gay, and it should be no different after."

FIND OUT MORE ON THE INTERNET

Parents, Families and Friends of Lesbians and Gays.
www.pflag.org

READ MORE ABOUT IT

Gold, Mitchell and Mindy Drucker. *Crisis: 40 Stories Revealing the Personal, Social, and Religious Pain of Growing Up Gay in America*. New York: Greenleaf, 2008.

Patterson, Romaine and Patrick Hinds. *The Whole World Was Watching: Living in the Light of Matthew Shepard*. Los Angeles: Advocate Books, 2005.

Swigonski, Mary E., Robin Mama, and Kelly Ward. *From Hate Crimes to Human Rights*. New York: Routledge, 2001.

BIBLIOGRAPHY

Berger, R. "Passing: Impact on the Quality of Same-Sex Couple Relationships." Department of Social Work, California State University, 1990.

Denizet-Lewis, Benoit. "Coming Out in Middle School." *New York Times,* September 23, 2009.

Elias, Marilyn. "Gay Teens Coming Out Earlier to Peers and Family." *USA Today,* February 11, 2007.

Jacobs, Ethan. "New Study Shows Power of Parental Acceptance, Rejection." *Bay Windows,* January 8, 2009.

Jordan, K.; Deluty, R. "Coming Out for Lesbian Women: Its Relation to Anxiety, Positive Affectivity, Self-Esteem, and Social Support." Department of Psychology, DePaul University, 1998.

Keith, Bill. "A Man's Man." *Out,* August 2008.

Klein, Julia M. "Change of Heart: Older Adults Coming Out of the Closet Late in Life." *AARP Bulletin Today,* August 21, 2008.

Landau, Elizabeth. "Coming Out Late in Life Is Complex, but Not Unusual." *CNN,* December 11, 2009.

Owens, Tom. "One Mother's Voice: PFLAG Cofounder Recalls Group's Beginnings." Tolerance.org, July 14, 2005.

Staff. "Neil Patrick Harris 'I Am a Very Content Gay Man'." *People,* November 20, 2006.

INDEX

adolescence 14
American Medical Association 21

Children of Lesbians and Gays Everywhere (COLAGE) 22
Christian 39, 41, 48
the closet 23, 35, 42

Degeneres, Betty 52
Degeneres, Ellen 17, 52
depression 21, 30–32
DiFranco, Ani 10

Eichberg, Rob 10
employee resource groups (ERGs) 57

Gay, Lesbian, and Straight Education Network (GLSEN) 37
gay pride 12, 13, 47, 57
gay-straight alliance (GSA) 17, 35

Harris, Neil Patrick 58
hate crimes 18–20
homeless 20, 25
homophobia 25
Human Rights Campaign (HRC) 10, 12, 19 54, 56

Indigo Girls 10

Johns Hopkins Sexual Behaviors Consultation Unit 22, 41

LGBT 9
liberal 16

March on Washington for Lesbian and Gay Rights 10, 11
Martin, Ricky 26–28
mentor 32, 46

National Coming Out Day 9, 11, 52
National Gay and Lesbian Task Force 20

O'Leary, Jean 10
Outlet Program 30

Parents, Families and Friends of Lesbians and Gays (PFLAG) 19, 35, 51, 54

Resource Guide to Coming Out 12
RuPaul 10

Seniors Active in a Gay Environment (SAGE) 22

sin 39, 40
Stipe, Michael 10
Straight Guide to GLBT Americans 54
suicide 21, 30, 31

therapist 20, 22, 32, 34

Wainwright, Rufus 10

ABOUT THE AUTHOR AND THE CONSULTANT

Jaime A. Seba's involvement in LGBT issues began in 2004, when she helped open the doors of the Pride Center of Western New York, which served a community of more than 100,000 people. As head of public education and outreach, she spearheaded one of the East Coast's first crystal methamphetamine awareness and harm reduction campaigns. She also wrote and developed successful grant programs through the Susan G. Komen Breast Cancer Foundation, securing funding for the region's first breast cancer prevention program designed specifically for gay, bisexual, and transgender women. Jaime studied political science at Syracuse University before switching her focus to communications with a journalism internship at the *Press & Sun-Bulletin* in Binghamton, New York, in 1999. She is currently a freelance writer based in Seattle.

James T. Sears specializes in research in lesbian, gay, bisexual, and transgender issues in education, curriculum studies, and queer history. His scholarship has appeared in a variety of peer-reviewed journals and he is the author or editor of twenty books and is the Editor of the *Journal of LGBT Youth*. Dr. Sears has taught curriculum, research, and LGBT-themed courses in the departments of education, sociology, women's studies, and the honors college at several universities, including: Trinity University, Indiana University, Harvard University, Penn State University, the College of Charleston, and the University of South Carolina. He has also been a Research Fellow at Center for Feminist Studies at the University of Southern California, a Fulbright Senior Research Southeast Asia Scholar on sexuality and culture, a Research Fellow at the University of Queensland, a consultant for the J. Paul Getty Center for Education and the Arts, and a Visiting Research Lecturer in Brazil. He lectures throughout the world.